D0834052

To:- Vera Muggeridge.

Can you tell me yet when you'll
be coming home? Or, have you found
your caravan rests in a new place.

I hope you'll like most of these
poems especially the spring and
country ones. We can look forward to
a better new year in 1990. Godwilling.

Love x Ruth &   x Grace
            Kane   Head.

261 CROYDON ROAD
CATERHAM VALLEY
SURREY CR3 6PG.

Tele:- 0883-344416

The Fireside Book

A picture and a poem
for every mood
chosen by

David Hope

Printed and Published by
D. C. THOMSON & CO., LTD.,
185 Fleet Street, London EC4A 2HS.
ISBN 0 85116 458 7

COUNTRY-CUM-CITY

DON'T ask me, please, to choose between
    Fair countryside and town,
'Twixt Norman towers,
Old churchyard bowers,
And harebell's soft blue gown:
'Tween country days with country ways,
Windflowers in the dell;
Rabbits and bees,
Laburnum trees,
Wild gorse and sweet briar smell:

Or city closes, bustling streets,
Stall traders in the square,
Steeples and clocks,
Crescents and blocks,
A busker's wheedling air . . .
For I'll walk down the open roads,
Thro' winding alleys stroll —
Happy and free
In mood I'll be
While I applaud them all!

Mary M. Milne

THE PILGRIMS' WAY

OH, the little lane led me such a dance,
  Over the hill and down,
But I still kept on, so glad to be
Out in the sunshine, fancy-free,
Away from the clamour of town.

Unchanged, for a thousand years or more,
Past hedges creamy with may,
Through bramble-thickets, and banks of fern,
And dim green woods, it would twist and turn,
As it followed its hallowed way.

For long ago, in the mists of time,
When faith burned bright as a flame,
This old path led to a holy shrine,
And here, imbued with a love divine,
The gentle pilgrims came.

The lane is almost forgotten now,
(Though guide-books list it still),
But sometimes, soft on the blossomy air,
There echoes a fragment of ancient prayer,
As if the sanctity lingers there
Like a blessing, and always will . . .

Kathleen O'Farrell

YESTERDAY

JUST yesterday, when I was young,
  And all my songs were still unsung,
I met a girl with eyes a-shine
And dreamed that she'd be mine.

An Autumn hush becalmed each street,
The hours danced by on careless feet;
I'd heard it said that love is blind,
And yet she seemed so kind.

The sun dipped low, and then was gone,
Above the town a bright star shone;
I offered her a young man's heart —
She said we had to part.

Ah, dreams of youth, they're fairy gold!
How swift they fade, when love turns cold.
But I remember eyes of grey,
And smile at yesterday.

Peter Cliffe

HIGHLAND BAY

AH, here is peace: the lazy tides that rise
   In shallow steps that scarcely find their way;
The nearer, green, the deeper, blue, that lies
   Beyond the sea-birds rocking on the bay;
Ah, here is peace, and here the happy day.

Amid the urgent beat and stress of time,
   The anxious hours, the striving and the strain,
Shall memory evoke this quiet clime
   And taste its sweet serenity again;
The tranquil tides shall make an end of pain.

Averil Stewart

AUTUMN

GIVE me the woods on an Autumn day —
  The late bloom and the berry,
The yellow leaf on an outstretched branch,
  The wind-borne leaves of the cherry.

Show me a path where the bracken rears
  Its fronds of yellow and brown,
And a shimmering bank of willow-herb
  Like a cloud when the sun's gone down.

Give me the peace of an Autumn day
  With sounds all muted and sweet,
The sinking sun aglow through the trees,
  Soft moss beneath my feet.

And best of all, the twilight hour
  When mists drift tenderly,
To quench at last with lingering kiss
  The embers of the day.

Victorine Buttberg

THE POACHER'S LAMENT

WITHOUT a doubt I've tickled trout,
    And bagged a bird or two,
I've even made a habit of catching me a rabbit,
To make into an appetising stew.
More than once I have been caught,
and have had to go to court,
Where the magistrate is very strict indeed;
He listens to my tale,
Then he threatens me with gaol,
If I'm brought before him once again to plead.
But I'm much too old these days
For the mending of my ways,
And I'm sure to chance my luck again quite soon,
As there's nothing more delicious,
Than the taste of fresh cooked fishes,
Which you've caught yourself beneath a waning
    moon.
I've been a poacher all my life,
I even poached my wife —
From a fellow who was better off than I,
For although I lacked his wealth,
I made up for this with stealth
As I wooed her from him with my poacher's eye.
I can poach most anything,
From a pheasant to a ling,
I've even poached a hare with bandy legs,
But alas! and O alack!
I just do not have the knack
Of the supreme art of poaching common eggs!

Jon de-Colray

NO CHOICE!

SOMETIMES, rather wistfully,
    I think it might be fun
To choose a kitten for myself,
    A very special one.
For though I'm very fond of cats,
    Each colour, every sort,
I've never had the option of
    A long-haired or a short.

For strays have always made their way
    Unbidden, to my door,
Ginger, and grey, and tortoiseshell,
    And jet-black cats galore.
Bedraggled, in the pouring rain,
    Half-frozen, in the snow,
Who could turn away a cat
    With nowhere else to go?

Dear Bunty, Blackie, Tabby-Tom,
    And all their furry kin,
Some were very beautiful,
    Some battle-scarred and thin,
But when their sad eyes gazed at me,
    With such a mute despair,
I'd let these lesser brethren in,
    Our hearth and home to share.

And each one, in its turn, became
    A cherished family pet,
Smooth, or fluffy, spotted, striped,
    All lovable — and yet,
Although for countless years, I've had
    A cat upon my knee,
I've never chosen one of them,
    They've always chosen me!

Kathleen O'Farrell

WINTER COMES

THE epitaph of Autumn, traced in leaves,
  Fades in the snow.

See, guarding still imaginary sheaves,
  Yon old scarecrow!

Along the skyline, white against white skies,
  The mountains mass,

Until, grey shades amid the dusk, they rise
  And softly pass

Into the deeper night, and darkly stand
  Transformed again

As Winter, the new tenant in the land,
  Takes all the glen.

Malcolm K. MacMillan

THE LAST OVER

BATSMAN batting,
  Bowler bowling,
Now appealing—" How was that?"
Umpire watching,
Quickly scotching,
" No, it did not hit the bat!"

Fine leg finer,
Cover squarer,
Six to win, one mighty clout.
Batsman sweating,
Bowler fretting,
" Will I never get him out?"

Last man facing,
Bowler racing,
" Pitch it up, don't drop one short."
Willow crashing,
Leather flashing,
To the boundary——" Is he caught?"

Long leg hopping,
Chance of dropping
This most vital catch of all.
Fingers stinging,
Voices ringing,
Safely pouched, that leather ball.

J. M. Anthony

THE OLD PARISH CHURCH, WHITBY

WE climbed the steep where headless Edwin
  lies —
The king who struck for Christ, and striking fell;
Beyond the harbour tolled the beacon bell;
Saint Mary's peal sent down her glad replies;
So entered we the church: white galleries,
Cross-stanchions, frequent stairs, dissembled well
A ship's mid-hold, — we almost felt the swell
Beneath, and caught o'erhead the sailors' cries.

But as we heard the congregational sound,
And reasonable voice of common prayer
And common praise, new wind was in our sails —
Heart called to heart, beyond the horizon's bound
With Christ we steered, through angel-haunted air,
A ship that meets all storms, rides out all gales.

Hardwick Rawnsley

A GARDEN

LOW through my heart like the musical mingling
  of fountains
And the laughter of moorland streams
Comes the lilt of a melody sweet with the musk of
  the roses
And the rich mellowness of ancient things.
I see again the twilight fall on a well-loved garden
And the sun's last blessing on the evening corn.
I feel again the quiet that would flood the meadows
After the stars were born.

Malcolm K. MacMillan

IN PENSIVE MOOD

I TOUCHED a full-bloomed rose today,
   Fresh bathed in Summer rain,
I breathed its fragrance — and I could
   But wonder whence it came.

I sat beneath a mighty tree —
   Cool shade from noonday sun,
In pensive mood I touched a leaf —
   And thought — whence had it come?

A bird upon the high treetop,
   How sweetly did it sing —
O mystery! What magic hand
   Had made this tiny thing?

The grass so soft beneath my feet —
   I marvelled at its green —
What artist's brush could e'er portray
   The vibrance of this scene?

And then I thought — how came these hills? —
   Such exquisite design!
How come the showers, the sunshine? Ah!
   'Tis all the hand divine.

                    Patricia McGavock

COUNTRY VOICES

I CAN hear them once again,
    Through the murmur of the rain,
Calling to me down the years,
Till my eyes are filled with tears;
And the treasured memories start:
Country voices in my heart.

Now the Winter nights are long
And no blackbird trills his song,
Come those voices once I knew —
Childhood skies were ever blue!
Soft and tender, warm and kind:
Country voices in my mind.

Bedtime tales of old romance,
In the firelight shadow-dance;
Arms that held me if I wept,
Eyes that watched me while I slept.
Country voices, sweet and slow:
How I loved you long ago!

Peter Cliffe

MARCH WINDS

THE wind blows fresh, the wind blows free,
    It brings the thrill of Spring to me,
The clouds sail through the bright, blue sky,
All fleecy — dancing up on high,
And as I walk along the street,
The wind would lift me from my feet.

The wind blows keen, the wind blows through
My overcoat and jacket, too,
It takes the petals from the trees
And chases round the roofs and eaves
Of every cottage in the lane,
As though it played some impish game.

I love the wind that comes to play
Along our streets this bright March day,
It quickens thought in my dull brain,
And wakes my heart to life again;
How joyous are the winds that bring
This first enchanting breath of Spring.

Margaret H. Dixon

THE WINDOW

TWO hats on show: one green, one blue;
  Spring hats for passers-by to view.
Their beauty somehow mocked the rain
That hissed and drenched the window-pane,
And helped my inner eye to see —
Lambs, catkins, buds upon the tree;
The swallow's swoop, the hawthorn braid
Like cream upon the hedgerow laid.
For though the Winter was the season,
The Spring was mine . . . those hats the reason!

Noel Scott

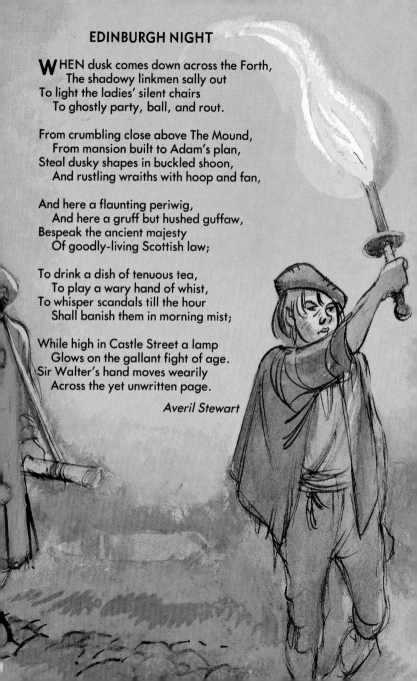

EDINBURGH NIGHT

WHEN dusk comes down across the Forth,
  The shadowy linkmen sally out
To light the ladies' silent chairs
  To ghostly party, ball, and rout.

From crumbling close above The Mound,
  From mansion built to Adam's plan,
Steal dusky shapes in buckled shoon,
  And rustling wraiths with hoop and fan,

And here a flaunting periwig,
  And here a gruff but hushed guffaw,
Bespeak the ancient majesty
  Of goodly-living Scottish law;

To drink a dish of tenuous tea,
  To play a wary hand of whist,
To whisper scandals till the hour
  Shall banish them in morning mist;

While high in Castle Street a lamp
  Glows on the gallant fight of age.
Sir Walter's hand moves wearily
  Across the yet unwritten page.

Averil Stewart

THE SKIRT

WAS it chance that sewed this peasant woman's
  skirt,
The full crimson rustling as she walks, and the broad
  blue
And ochre borders? Or was it just the dyes and
  stuffs she had to hand,
Bought for their cheapness? Or did she, with an
  artistry and skill
That knew so well her country and her soil, fashion
  it so? She who moved rhythmically,
Poising her rust-brown pitcher on her head
Or bending to dig the roots with bare fingers,
  broken nails,
Her metal bracelets falling on her wrists
And jangling at her ankles. Did she see the beauty?
  Did she starve and save
And then create it so? No, but as birds and squirrels
Know their colours, she knew hers: the redstart, the
  oriole, the blue jay;
Knew too, like them, the setting for her dark hair
And glowing eyes. Knew as the soil and Summer
  know their colours;
Knew as the fields know in their seasons what to
  wear.

Bryan Cave-Browne-Cave

DOWN GLO'STER WAY

THERE'S ploughing now, down Glo'ster way,
   An' apple-blossom blowin',
There's bonny lanes all white with may,
An' Severn silver flowin',
There's cheery creakin' of the plough,
An' peewits' cry, I'm knowin',
It's blue above the furrows now.
An' gulls are seaward goin'.

Oh, where the woods are wakin', there,
An' daisy buds are breaking there —
My way I would be taking there —
At home, down Glo'ster way;
I'm dreamin' of a flowery lane,
An' blossom wet with scented rain —
An' oh! that I were there again —
At home, down Glo'ster way!

There's sowin' now, down Glo'ster way,
An' whistle in the mornin',
There's sun a-smilin' on the ley,
An' kindly goes the corn in,
Oh, there's my heart, down Glo'ster way;
An' tho' it's long to reapin',
I'd bring my sheaves at close of day,
An' rest me there for sleepin'.

Oh, waitin', dreamin' countryside,
Where once the peewits wheeled and cried —
God give me back at eventide
My home down Glo'ster way!
Where cool the wind goes sighin' there,
An' gulls come inland flyin' there,
I'd sleep more peaceful lyin' there —
In earth, down Glo'ster way!

Anne Page

THE ROAD

ON either hand the meadows lie
   Golden and grey and green,
And far away to the edge of the sky
   The white road runs between.
The meadows lie on either hand
   Golden and green and grey,
And the road runs on to a magic land,
   Wonderful, far away.
If some good fairy would give me wings
   And teach me the way to fly,
I would go to look for beautiful things
   Where the white road meets the sky.

I look at the fields and the road all day,
   And when I'm in bed at night,
I dream I'm ever so far away
   On the road by candlelight.
And I see all sorts of wonderful things,
   Castles and crystal streams,
Beautiful ladies and queens and kings —
   But then it is only dreams.
Yet — dragons and giants and princes tall,
   Witches and rugs that fly —
I'm quite, quite sure we should find them all
   Where the white road meets the sky.

Herbert Kennedy

BUTTERFLIES OF LULWORTH

SHY fairies live on Bindon Hill
  And gather nectar where they will.
Fluttering, fragile pinion hue
Brush yellow trefoil, scabious blue,
To sprinkle stardust as they fly,
Bewitching curious, watchful eye.

Adonis Blue and Lulworth Skipper
Weave a spell on casual tripper,
In sun and flowers, drift to sleep
On ancient soil, round and steep,
Above the shimmering, secret cove,
This magic place where fairies rove.

Kathryn L. Garrod

AU REVOIR TO BOOKS

TO black and red, yellow and blue,
   Green and umber, I bid adieu;
I raise my hat and I say goodbye:
I'm off to the green fields under the sky.

No ill-will, though; no ill-will;
We part for the nonce, but I love you still;
I love you still, my dear old friends,
And will love right through till the world ends.

But, good old souls, Spring's here again:
Primroses pale in thicket and glen,
Violets hidden and windflowers bold,
And a million catkins dusty with gold.

You're dead dumb, but the pastures bleat
With the voices of lambs on capering feet,
And the cuckoo's back from over the seas,
And the air is loud with the hum of bees.

And birds are pairing, and Life and Love
Are billing and cooing like dove and dove;
And the thing's in my head; so I'm off; good-bye;
I'm away to the green fields under the sky.

Latimer McInnes

NANCIBELLA

NANCIBELLA loved to tease,
    She drove the young men crazy,
Yet it was her they sought to please,
    Not gentle sister Daisy.

Nancibella hated toil,
    Dreamy she was, and lazy,
Yet everybody chose to spoil
    Sweet Nancy — never Daisy.

For Nancy, she was prettier far
    Than Molly, Madge, or Maisie,
Like candles they, and she a star,
    And all outshone dear Daisy.

To see her long black lashes curl,
    Would constantly amaze me,
Oh, Nancy was a lovely girl,
    Not freckle-faced like Daisy!

Dear Nancibella — through my song
    I so delight to praise thee,
For I will love you all life long,
    And so will my wife, Daisy!

Kathleen O'Farrell

IDLING

I'M idling in the garden shed,
    Listening to the rain,
The roof is drumming overhead,
    The earth can breathe again;
The thirsty vegetables outside
    Imbibe the welcome drops,
So now I have myself stopped work
    To drink until it stops.

I'll rest upon this tattered rug,
    Lean on a pile of sand,
And very soon I'll hold a mug
    Of cider in my hand.
In order that I shall not be
    Disturbed by bark or shout,
I'll open wide the door to see,
    And keep a sharp look out.

And here I'll eat my bread and cheese,
    And true contentment's mine.
I glance at blooming apple trees,
    They glisten and they shine;
A rainbow spans the nearby wood
    Beyond the garden wall,
And somewhere near, in solitude,
    The Maytime cuckoos call.

Glynfab John

THE LITTLE SHEPHERDESS

UPON Great-Granny's mantelpiece,
  There stands, in pride of place,
A dainty Dresden shepherdess
  With such a charming face.
A lamb is cradled in her arms,
  And round her pearly toes,
Her panniered skirt falls, full and red,
  Just like a damask rose.
Sometimes I stand and gaze at her,
  But now and then I dare
To lift her down, so carefully,
  And stroke her flaxen hair.
They say she's made of porcelain,
  And fragile as a flower,
But she's as real as you and me
  When midnight strikes the hour.
For sometimes, in that silvery hush,
  When I should be asleep,
I'm sure I hear my shepherdess
  Call softly to her sheep . . .

Kathleen O'Farrell

THE LILAC TREE

WHEN April leans from laughing skies
    To kiss the lilac tree,
A tender little tune shall rise
    To stir the heart of me.
And I will dream of scented rain
    One long-remembered Spring,
When lilac whispers once again
    The song I may not sing.

So many fragrant memories
    Of blossoms sweet and wet
Come dancing down the April breeze,
    And why should I forget?
Oh! I will wait the Winter long,
    And weary for the Spring,
To hear again the lilac-song
    That I may never sing.

Anne Page

THE BROOK

BROOK, happy brook, that glidest through my
  dell
And trippest with soft feet across the mead;
That, laughing on, a mazy course dost lead
O'er pebble beds, and reeds, and rushy swell;
Go by that cottage where my love doth dwell.
Ripple thy sweetest ripple, sing the best
Of melodies thou hast; lull her to rest
With such sweet tales as thou dost love to tell.
Say, "One is sitting in your wood tonight,
O maiden rare, to catch a glimpse of you;
A shadow fleet, or but a window-light,
Shall make him glad, and thrill his spirit through."
Brook, happy brook, I pray, go lingering,
And underneath the rosy lattice sing.

Thomas Ashe

HEAVEN

WE'VE a little thatched cottage,
  My Harry and me,
It's set on a hill
  At the rise of the lea;
There's a garden in front
  With an ancient yew tree,
And there's nowhere on earth
  Where I'd rather be.

In Springtime the bulbs
  Make a splendid display,
While the roses in June
  All my efforts repay;
The apple trees give us
  Fresh fruit every day
And our hens do their bit
  With the eggs that they lay.

The view from our house
  Is a sight to behold,
A patchwork of fields
  In the heart of the wold
And often, with Harry,
  The lanes I have strolled,
Watching each season's
  Fresh pageant unfold.

It may not seem much,
    But to me it's a lot,
I couldn't want more
    And I'll tell you what—
I'm grateful to God
    For this heaven I've got
With Harry, the cottage,
    And our little plot.

Elizabeth Bloomfield

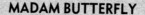

MADAM BUTTERFLY

SHE wafts and weaves 'mong scented stocks,
   Flits blithely o'er tall hollyhocks:
Alights but briefly — soars to pass
Pale waving fronds of Pampas grass.
On poppies red and wild bluebell
She settles, for the briefest spell:
On yellow broom, with folded wings
She, only for a moment, swings.

Sweet honeysuckle bids her stay,
Pink roses beckon her their way:
Gold kingcups, rosemary and rue —
She's undecided which to woo.

Life's such a whirl! Long Summer hours
Spent seeking out the prettiest flowers:
She'll kiss them lightly, passing by —
That coquette, Madam Butterfly.

Mary M. Milne

CARILLON

CHIME! Chime! from a bygone time,
  Bells of my youth!
  Love, beauty and truth,
Carillon of life in its prime.

Chime! Chime! What a song sublime
  Did the lark outpour!
  See, an open door,
A path, and a hill to climb.

Chime! Chime! Did the scent of the lime
  Waft the sound this way,
  From a far-off day,
O'er the silent wastes of time?

Anne MacDonald

THE OLD JOCKEY

HIS last days linger in that low attic
  That barely lets out the night,
With its gabled window on Knackers' Alley
  Just hoodwinking the light.

He comes and goes by that gabled window
  And then on the window-pane
He leans, as thin as a bottled shadow—
  A look, and he's gone again:

Eyeing, maybe, some fine fish-women
  In the best shawls of the Coombe
Or, maybe, the knife-grinder plying his treadle,
  A run of sparks from his thumb!

But, oh, you should see him gazing, gazing
  When solemnly out on the road
The horse drays pass overladen with grasses,
  Each driver lost in his load;

Gazing until they return; and suddenly,
  As galloping by they race,
From his pale eyes, like glass breaking,
  Light leaps on his face.

F. R. Higgins

HE — who offers his love
   Like a still, misty morn
Rising to a sun-kissed sky,
   I love.

He — who welcomes with a smile,
Warm and gentle as a rose,
The symbol of deepest love,
   I love.

He — who shows his caring
In little things — a book,
Flowers fresh from our garden,
   I love.

He — who understands, accepting,
Asking for nothing but
To share with me his love,
   I love.

Kathryn L. Garrod

AT THE BARBER'S

THE little old man put on his hat
    (I thought: " One day I'll be like that!")
The little old man walked wearily out
("Preserve me, Lord, from growing stout.")
The little old man went lonely away
(" Let me glimpse again—I'm going grey!")
With his shrivelled head and his sunken eye,
(" I'm not so sure but I'd rather die
While my legs are firm and my hair is thick—
The thought of depending on a stick!")
And I thought, " Make hay, son, while you can;
One day you'll be only a little old man."

Sydney Bell

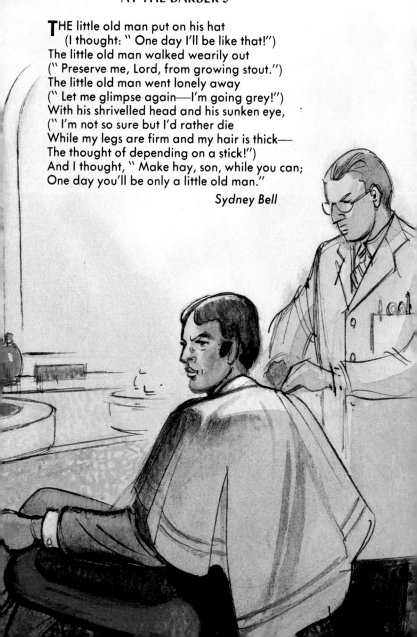

HIGHLANDERS

I LOVE the beasts of Highland breed —
   The beasts that served the ancient need
Of lonely shieling by the shaw
   And clachan 'neath the ben;
So shaggy, sober, douce and wise,
With powerful horns and patient eyes,
The same that Bonnie Charlie saw
   As he rode down the glen.

Let others boast the Beltie strain
Or Ayrshire herd for gear or gain;
For me the race of Celtic song,
   The cattle of the hill.
And, fathered by a Shorthorn bull,
The calves will fill my pockets full.
The breed shall bide where they belong —
   And I'll be Highland still.

Averil Stewart

THE ROSE

THE Rose in the garden slipped her bud,
    And she laughed in the pride of her youthful
      blood
As she thought of the Gardener standing by—
" He is old—so old! And he soon must die!"

The full Rose waxed in the warm June air,
And she spread and spread till her heart lay bare;
And she laughed once more as she heard his
    tread—
" He is older now! He will soon be dead!"

But the breeze of the morning blew, and found
That the leaves of the blown Rose strewed the
    ground;
And he came at noon, that Gardener old,
And he raked them gently under the mould.

And I wove the thing to a random rhyme,
For the Rose is beauty, the Gardener, Time.

                Austin Dobson

COACHING IN SCOTLAND

WHERE have I been this perfect Summer day —
    Or *fortnight* is it, since I rose from bed,
Devoured that kippered fish, the oatmeal bread,
And mounted to this box? O bowl away,
Swift stagers, through the dusk; I will not say
"Enough," nor care where I have been or be,
Nor know one name of hill, or lake, or lea,
Or moor, or glen! Were not the clouds at play
Nameless among the hills, and fair as dreams?
On such a day we must love things, not words,
And memory take or leave them as they are,
On such a day! What unimagined streams
Are in the world, how many haunts of birds,
What fields and flowers— and what an evening
    star!

Edward Dowden

TO JOCK

WHEN home my ship comes bringing
   A hundred pounds or more,
I'll buy an empty lighthouse
   That guards a lonely shore.

   There'll be no noisy tramcars,
     There'll be no daily news,
   You won't need your collar,
     And I shan't wear my shoes.

   You shall hunt for rabbits
     To fill the stewing-pot,
   While I will go a-fishing
     And think and dream a lot.

   You shall chase the seagulls
     And rouse the air with glee,
   While I will sniff salt breezes
     And write eternally.

   And when we're feeling homesick
     In fog and grey dull weather,
   We'll mount the top-most platform
     And sit and howl together.

Hylda C. Cole

THE BLACKBIRD

SOMEWHERE down the loaning there's a
    blackbird singing:
    What would be his theme now? Anyone could
        say!
And within my heart there's an echo ringing,
    Bringing me the mem'ry of a bygone day —

Of a bygone day, and a dear voice calling
    From the wee plantation where we loved to go.
Hawthorn in the hedges, and the blossom falling
    Light upon my cheek as the drifting snow —

As the drifting snow, or her lips, caressing,
    Telling me she loved me — but my eyes were
        blind
And I never knew 'til one day, confessing,
    Laughingly she told me. Was it really kind?

Was it really kind? Ah, my soul is singing
    Even tho' I'm old now, and the past is far away;
And within my heart there's the echo ringing,
    Like the blackbird's song on a bygone day.

Sydney Bell

GARRABOST

I'D never seen or heard of the place:
   asked a girl with a pretty face.
She looked on me as a creature lost:
"Yes, indeed, this is Garrabost;
And Bayable, of course, is farther south!"
A smile was hovering on her mouth.
She had surely met the most ignorant man
That ever had lived since the world began.
I smiled and thanked her. She smiled; went on;
And her milking pail in the sunset shone
All down the village, as twilight came
And hid the lassie and . . . What's-its-name?

Malcolm K. MacMillan

TRAVELLERS

I'M one of the travellin' Romany breed,
  Men call me Gypsy Joe;
I follow the roads where e'er they lead,
  And scorn the gorgio.

My hair is black as the wings o' night,
  And dark and keen my eye.
You'd best be sure you've the will to fight,
  Ere you name me diddekai.

My vardo wheels throw up the dust
  Through many a lonely day;
But I've found a chie to love and trust,
  And we'll wed in the Romany way.

She'll ride at my side each long day through,
  Sweetheart, wife and friend;
And we'll take our luck, as the Romanies do,
  Until our journey's end.

Peter Cliffe

FOUR AND SEVEN

WHEN you are safe in bed,
    And, for a while, no more
A piercing wrangle splits my head,
    Nor crash of banging door;
When o'er your quiet toys
    The moon a magic makes,
I sit and think, bereft of noise,
    And count up my mistakes.

I wonder, after all,
    If I am very wise,
You look so far-remote and small
    When sleep shuts down your eyes.
I think you play in dreams
    About the floors of Heaven,
And dabble in Elysian streams,
    Oh, little Four and Seven!

But in the everyday
    You need my guiding hand,
And what if I should let you stray,
    Or fail to understand?
Take all my hopes and fears
    And scraps of mother-lore,
Sleep, and forgive me, Seven-Years,
    And little Only-Four!

Anne Page

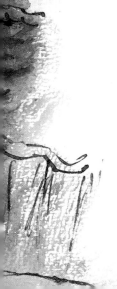

TIME

EVERY morning it deceives me,
   Every evening it intrigues me,
Tell me, someone — what is time?

Devised by man for simple reason:
The day, the hour, the changing season?
When to rise and when to sleep,
When to sow and when to reap?

A billion years — mere tick of history —
Just serves to aggravate the mystery.
'Tis said that time's the fourth dimension,
Which seems to me obscure pretension.

What else can we ascribe to time?
Ah, yes! Its sure affinity with crime;
Those naughty miscreants who've earned it,
And now regret they've had to serve it!

What more can we relate to time?
(Forgive me here, I needs must rhyme!)
We've those who save it, those who waste it . . .
But does it matter one small dime?

My brain's awhirl! It's time for bed.
I'll take my problems there instead,
And in my dreams Big Ben will chime,
Poor Ben — like me, a slave of time!

                              W. Carr

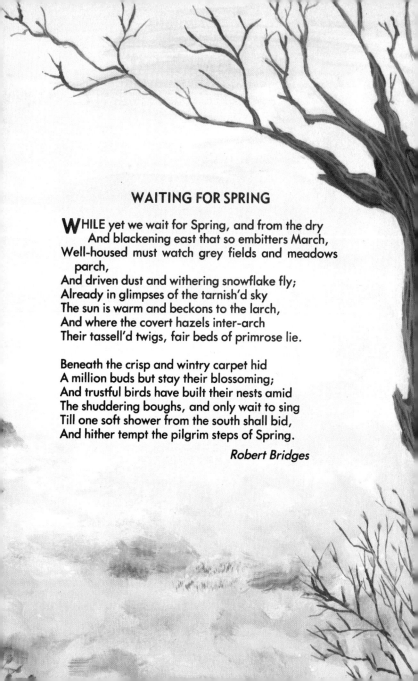

WAITING FOR SPRING

WHILE yet we wait for Spring, and from the dry
    And blackening east that so embitters March,
Well-housed must watch grey fields and meadows
    parch,
And driven dust and withering snowflake fly;
Already in glimpses of the tarnish'd sky
The sun is warm and beckons to the larch,
And where the covert hazels inter-arch
Their tassell'd twigs, fair beds of primrose lie.

Beneath the crisp and wintry carpet hid
A million buds but stay their blossoming;
And trustful birds have built their nests amid
The shuddering boughs, and only wait to sing
Till one soft shower from the south shall bid,
And hither tempt the pilgrim steps of Spring.

Robert Bridges

PATRICK'S LESSON

'TIS said there's a wee man in County Kildare,
   A leprechaun, small but unseen,
Who dances at night, by the moon's eerie light,
   On a certain old small village green.

It seems that he dances from midnight till dawn,
   And sings in a language unknown,
To the strains of a harp, somewhere in the park,
   Which plays away all on its own.

One night very late through the village there came,
   Mister Patrick O'Malley McShane,
Who'd been to the Inn, for a wee drop of gin,
   And had taken too much to his shame.

As he staggered along, resounding in song,
   Not caring a jot or a fig,
He looked to his right and beheld the rare sight
   Of a leprechaun dancing a jig.

So frightened was Pat that he fell on his back,
   And crossed himself several times over,
Whilst taking the chance of another feared glance
   At the spectacle there on the clover.

But to his surprise, when he opened his eyes,
   The vision had quite disappeared,
So a frightened McShane to his feet rose again,
   And fled like a man who'd been speared.

From then until now, our Pat's kept a vow
   Which he made to the Priest during Mass,
That no more would he sup, except tea from a cup
   Prepared by the hand of his lass.

Now to all you young fellows who drink to excess,
   Let this tale be a warning to care,
Lest on a fine night, you may witness the sight
   Of that leprechaun's dance in Kildare.

Jon de-Colray

THE WIND

WHAT a miracle wind is this
    Has crossed the English land to-day
With an unprecedented kiss,
    And wonderfully found a way!

Unsmirched incredibly and clean,
    Between the towns and factories,
Avoiding, has his long flight been,
    Bringing a sky like Sicily's.

O fine escape, horizon pure
    As Rome's! Black chimneys left and right
But not for him, the straight, the sure,
    His luminous day, his spacious night.

How keen his choice, how swift his feet!
    Narrow the way and hard to find!
This delicate stepper and discreet
    Walked not like any worldly wind.

Most like a man in man's own day,
    One of the few, a perfect one:
His open earth — the single way;
    His narrow road — the open sun.

Alice Meynell

OLD DAN AND I

HE came to me a tiny thing
    Of very tender age,
And lovingly I guarded him
    Through every growing stage;
He liked to have me throw him balls
    Which he'd retrieve, in play,
And chasing rabbits was his wont
    While I'd be making hay.

I taught him — 'twas no easy task—
    To bring the sheep to fold,
He'd turn them, in rebellious mood,
    Right back across the wold,
Yet when the snows so blinding
    Enclosed us like a shell,
Brave Dan would fetch the straylings
    Safely home o'er crag and fell.

Rough times and smooth together
    We've weathered, Dan and I,
But now the road grows steeper
    As evening draws on nigh,
We take our steps more slowly
    Yearning not for days long past,
And walk into the twilight,
    Companions to the last.

Mary M. Milne

RICHES ON A BARROW

WEATHERED old woman with your flower-
 seller's barrow,
 Are you April in disguise, your perfumed
 wares to bring?
Who but you could offer me, in squalid streets and
 narrow,
 The shining gold that's found on sunlit meadows
 in the Spring?

Choose not for me daffodils, though tall they are
 and slender;
 Not your gay anemones nor lilac now ablow;
Nor will I buy your tulips, for all their coloured
 splendour,
 But sell me your bright king-cups from the
 meadows that I know!

Back at home they'll tell me of the cuckoo-flowers adorning
    Fields where hawthorn and willow are breaking as of old;
Shall I dare to hesitate upon this April morning
    To swap a single silver piece for such a hoard of gold?

Glynfab John

HOMECOMING

THE loch lay agleam
    In the bright of the morn;
The wind was a dream
In the heart of the corn.

The road was a rainbow
All wet in the sun;
My cottage a castle;
My journey was done.

Malcolm K. MacMillan

OLD MAN

GIVE the old man his way. His years are tired of
time.
He's only a little longer now to climb the dales
Where his heart is: Shunner and Burtersett and the
tiered
Stone stairways of Moss Gill. Remember him that
day
On Lovely Seat, when the rime of the dark snow
wind
Caught at his beard, and how he looked: his hat
tipped
Backwards on his head; his hands crook'd on his
stick
And his eyes, wrinkled and bright, searching the
twisted
River a thousand feet below. And how the words
Formed on his lips and then, as fitting there,
Burst forth: Keats, Hopkins, Milton, Shakespeare.
And the sound, blown like a mighty music on the
wind,
Echoed and echoed down the valley, while you
and I
And all that hillside, could only stand and stare.

Bryan Cave-Browne-Cave

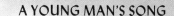

A YOUNG MAN'S SONG

MY girl is true, my girl is sweet,
　　When in the town we chance to meet
It almost seems to me as though
　　A rose were growing in the street.

And if I see her in the lane,
　　Though winter's freezing might and main,
I half suspect, in spite of all,
　　That Spring's upon us once again.

When luck is out and things look blue
　　And folks are up against me too,
There's naught in that to cast me down
　　Because she trusts me through and through.

And at the altar-railings when
　　My faith and truth I swear, oh then
I'll pray, " God strike me if I fail—
　　So help me! World without end. Amen!"

Violet Jacob

AN EVENING RETREAT

O LOVED wild hill-side, that hast been a power
    Not less than books, greater than preacher's
    art,
To heal my wounded spirit, and my heart
Retune to gentle thoughts, that hour on hour
Must languish in the city, like a flower
In wayside dust, while on the vulgar mart
We squander for scant gold our better part
From morn till eve, in frost, and sun, and shower!
My soul breaks into singing as I haste,
Day's labour ended, towards thy sylvan shrine
Of rustling beech, hawthorn, and eglantine;
And, wandering in thy shade, I dream of thee
As of green pastures 'mid the desert waste,
Wells of sweet water in the bitter sea.

David M. Main

ACKNOWLEDGEMENTS
We wish to thank the following for the use of their poems: Mary M. Milne, Peter Cliffe, Victorine Buttberg, Jon de-Colray, Patricia McGavock, Margaret H. Dixon, Noel Scott, Kathryn L. Garrod, Glynfab John, and Sydney Bell.